Wild World

a coloring book

by

Kate Fitzpatrick

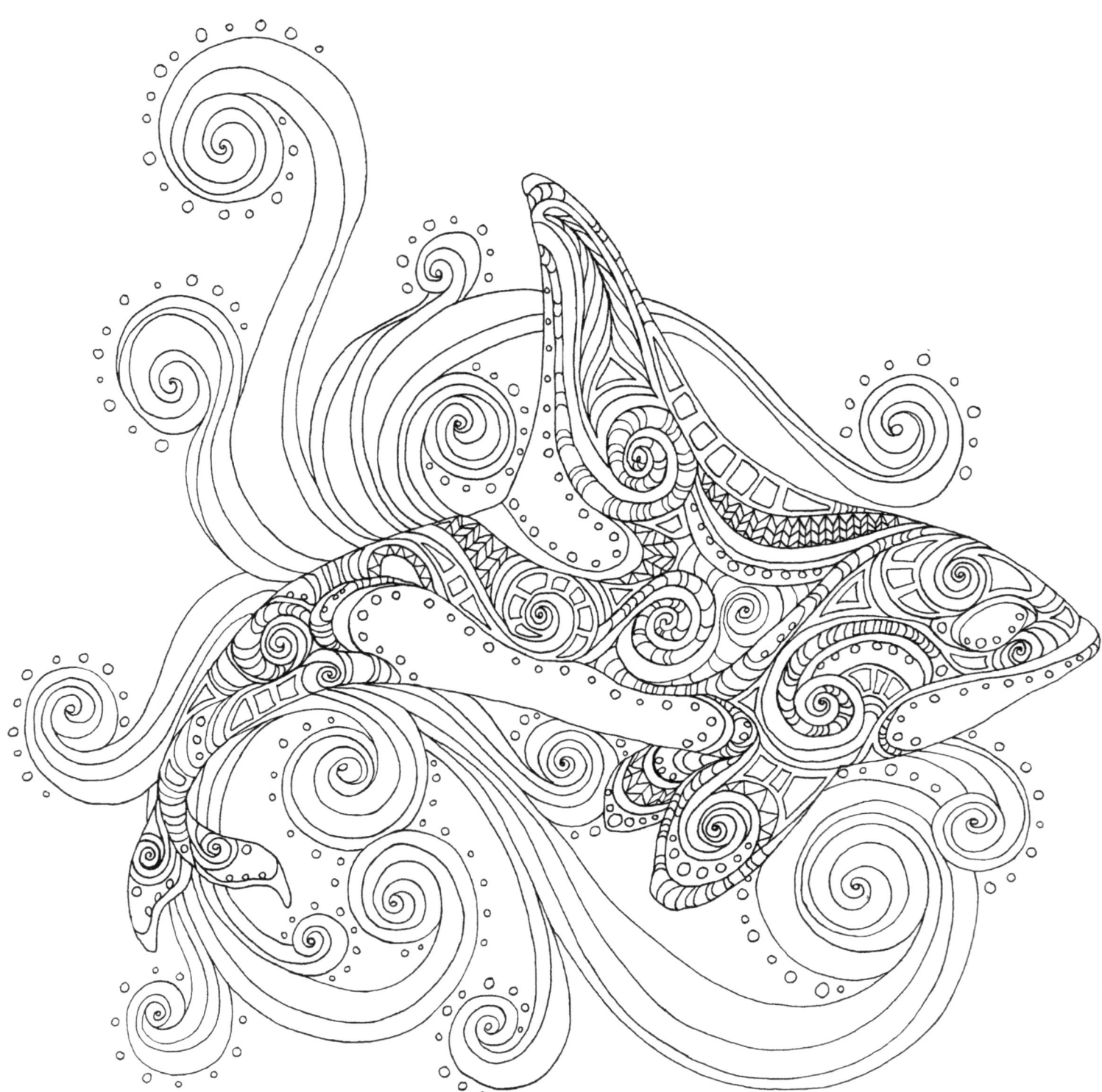

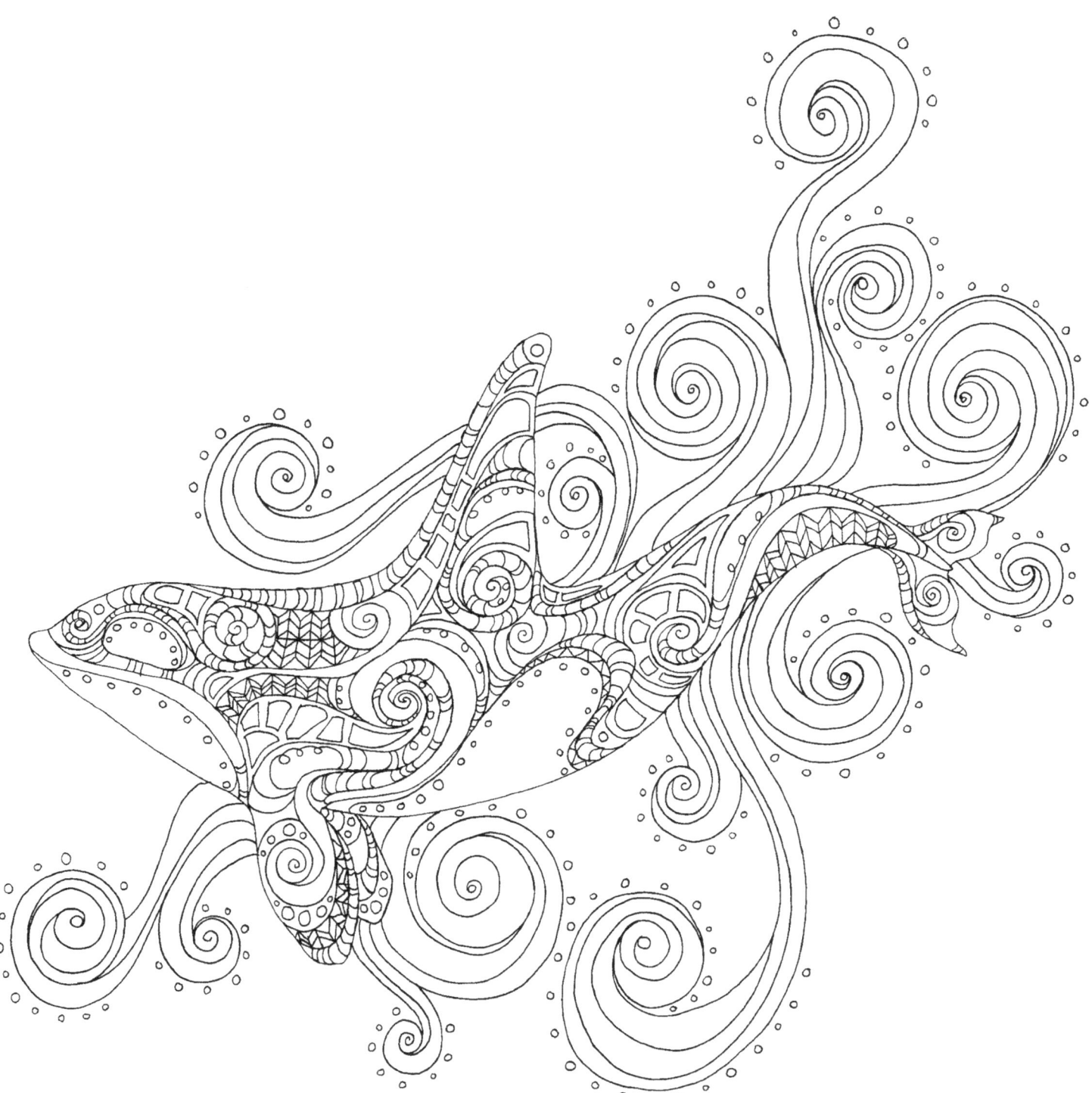

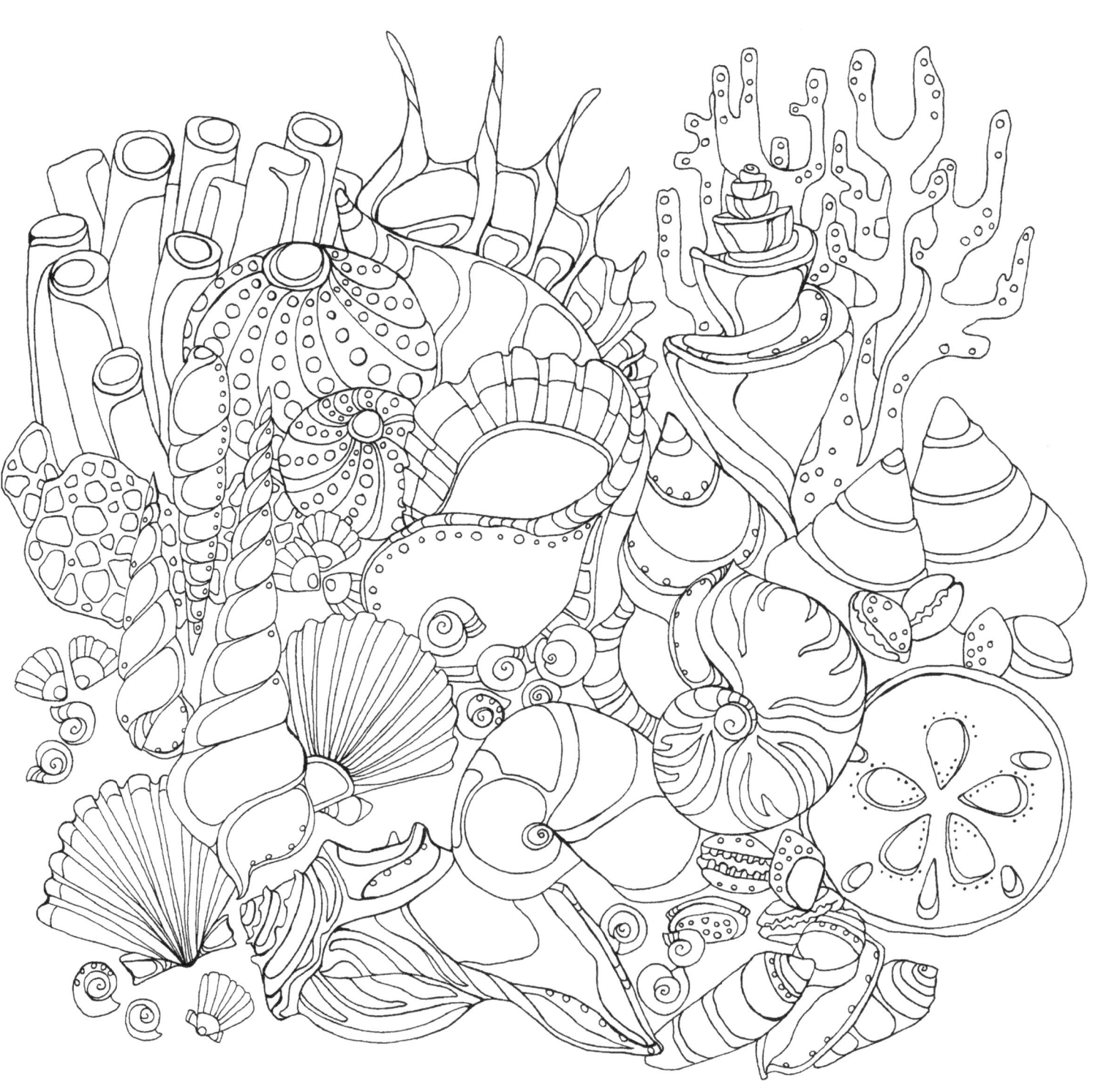

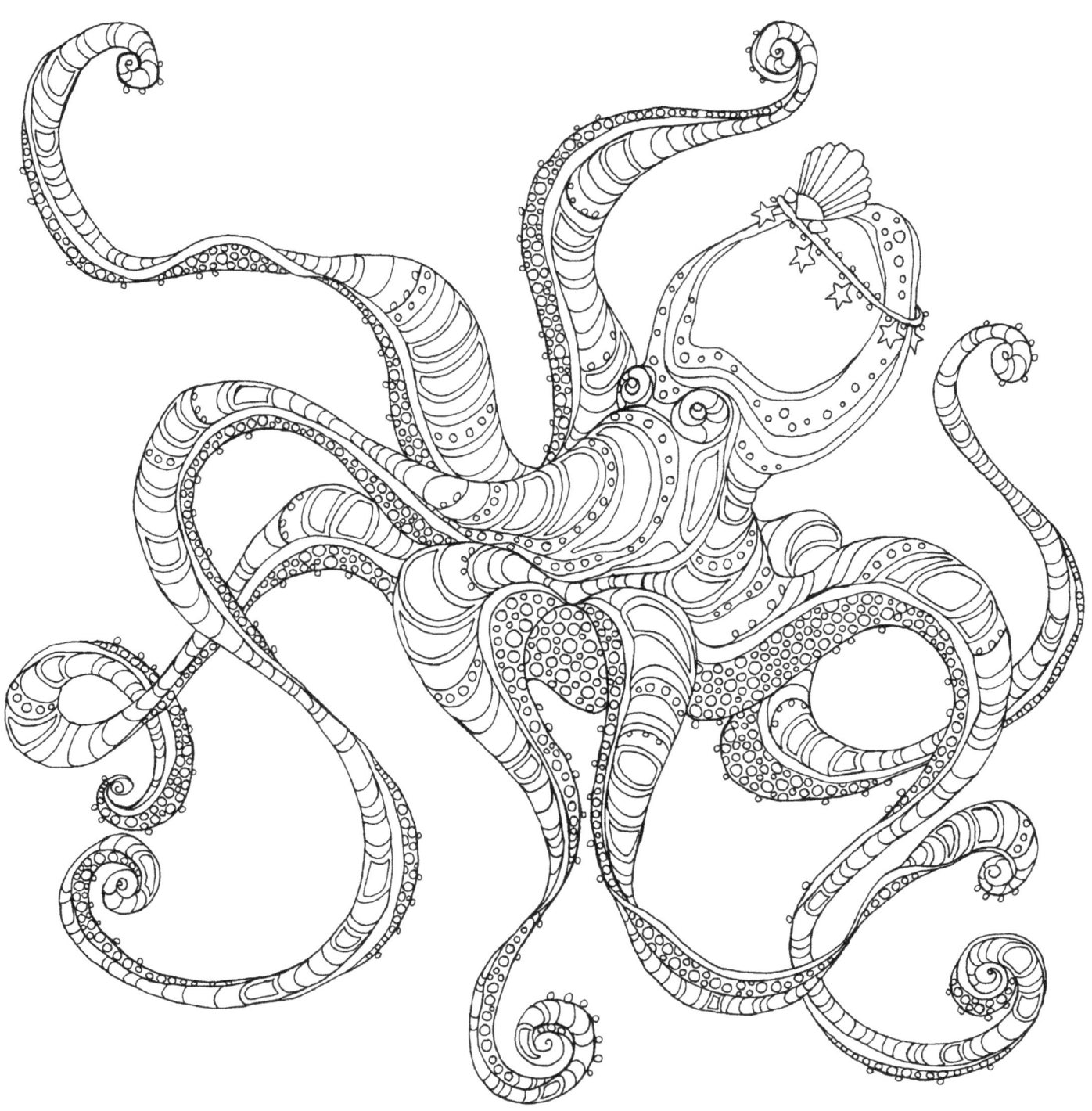

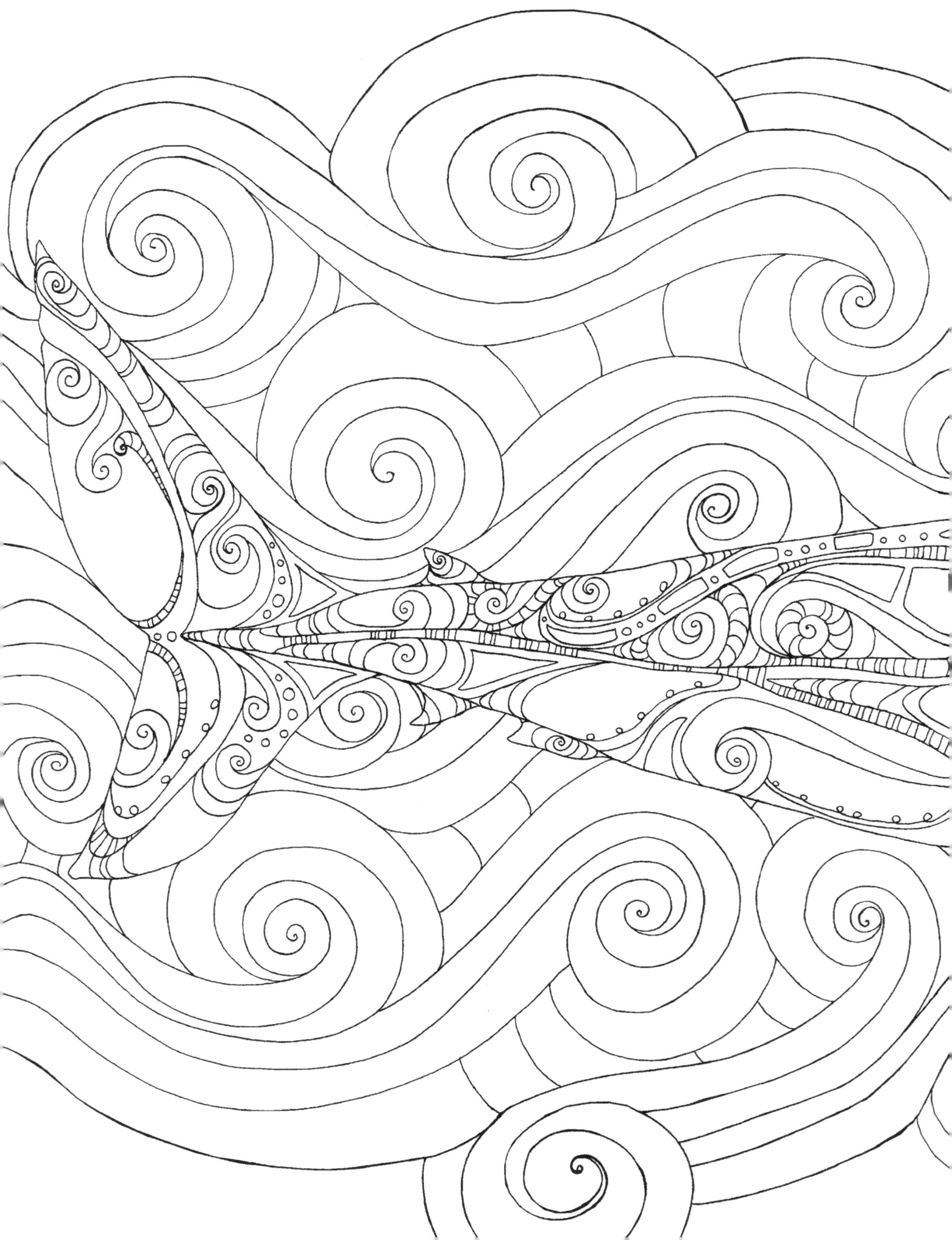

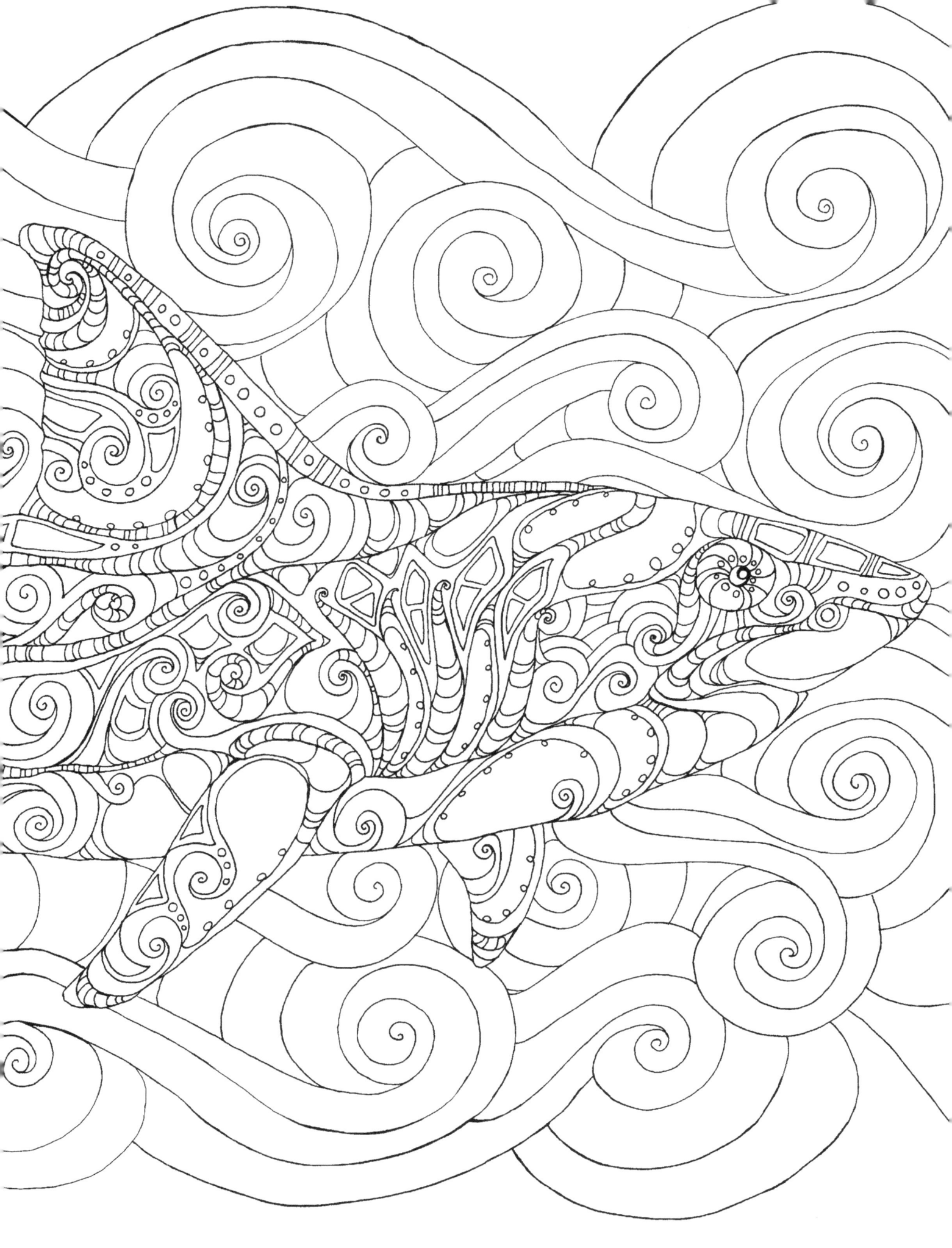

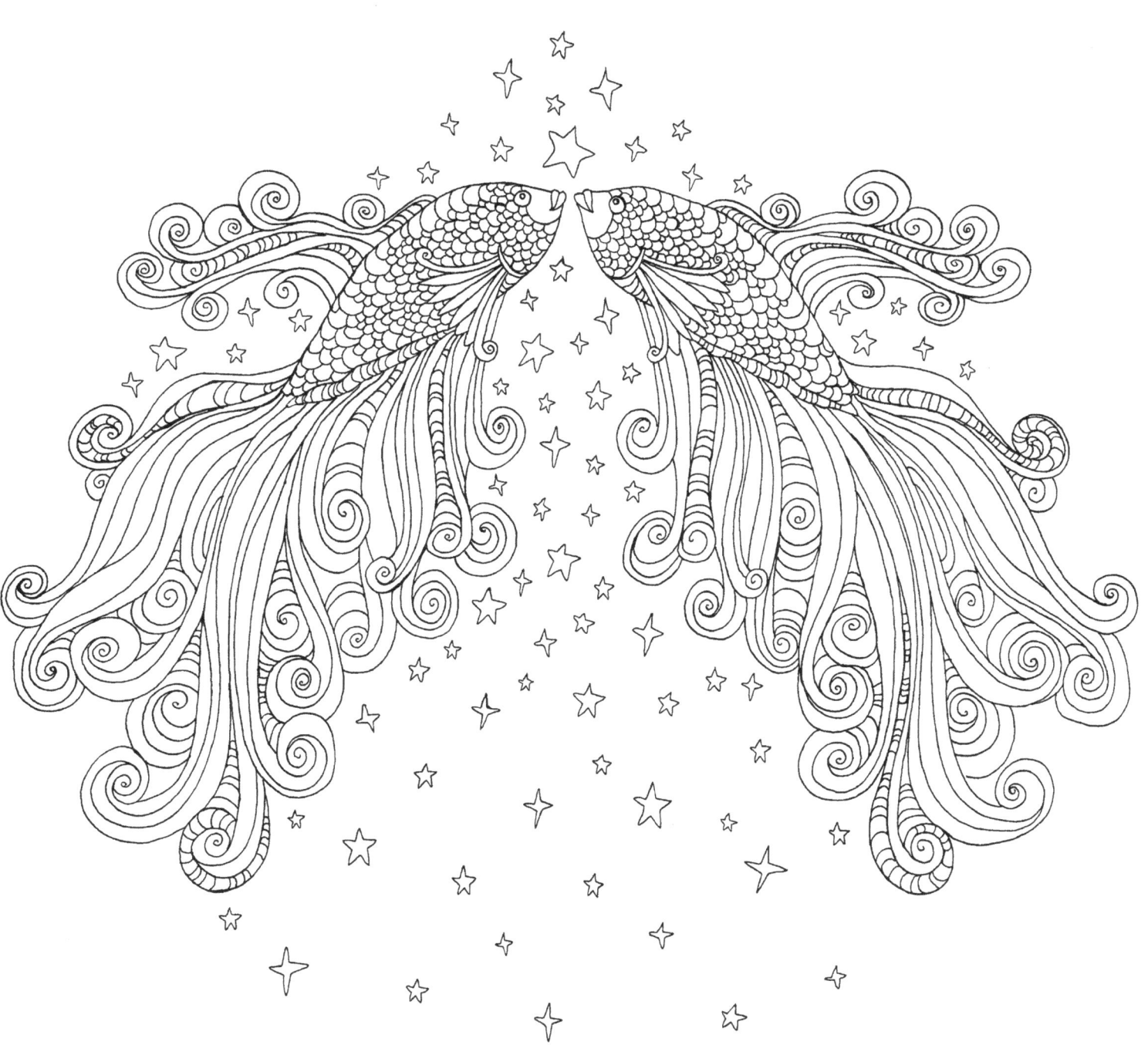

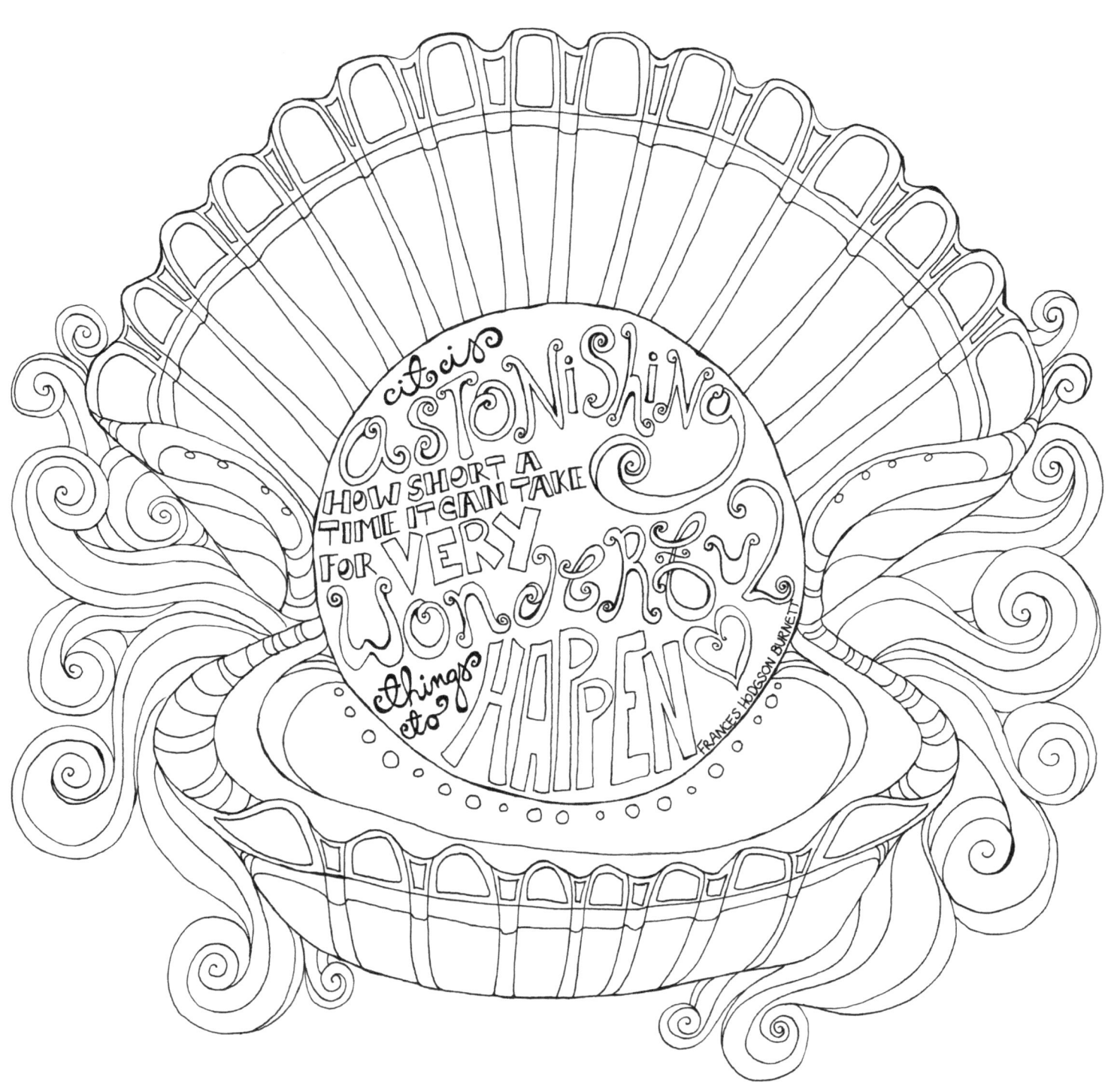

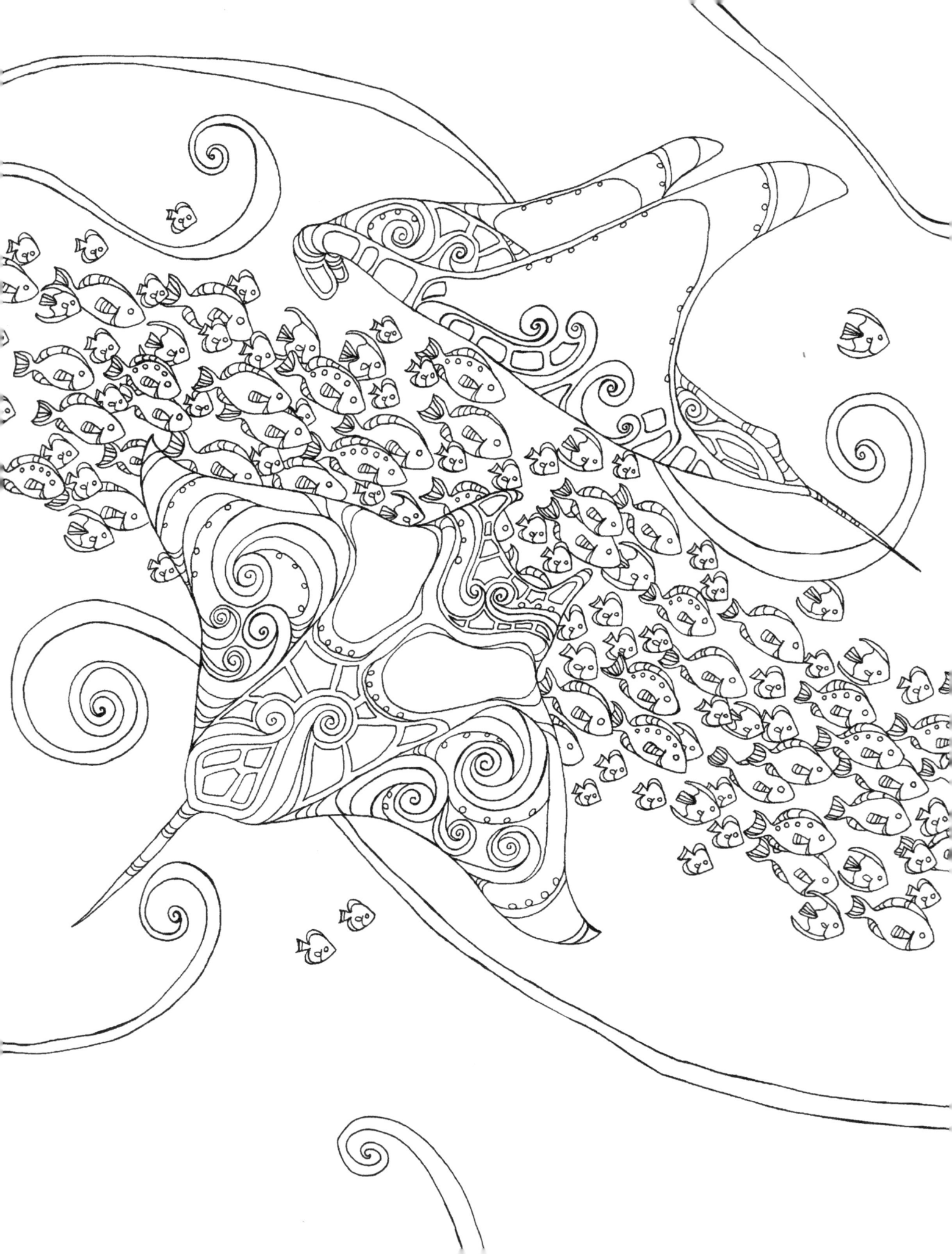

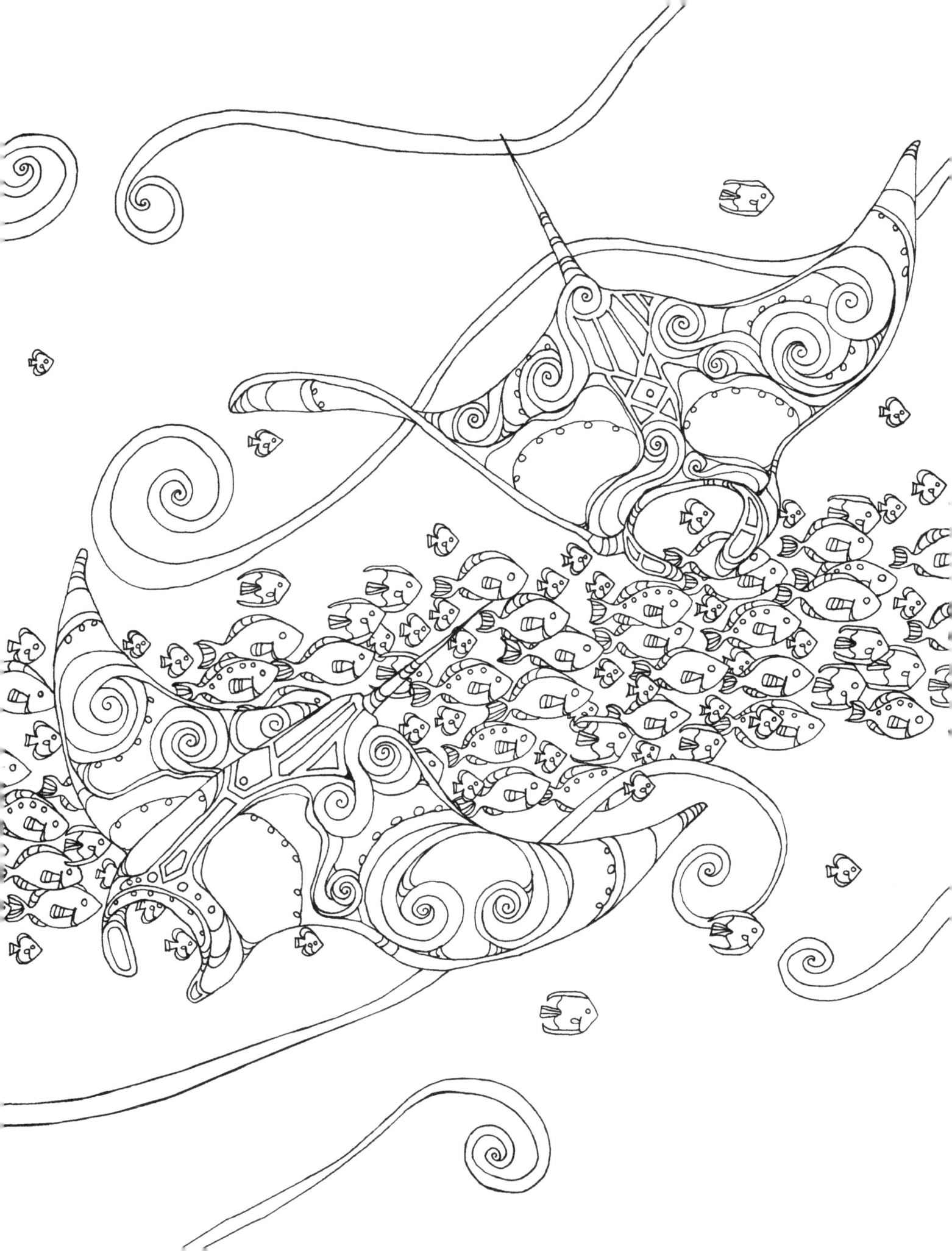

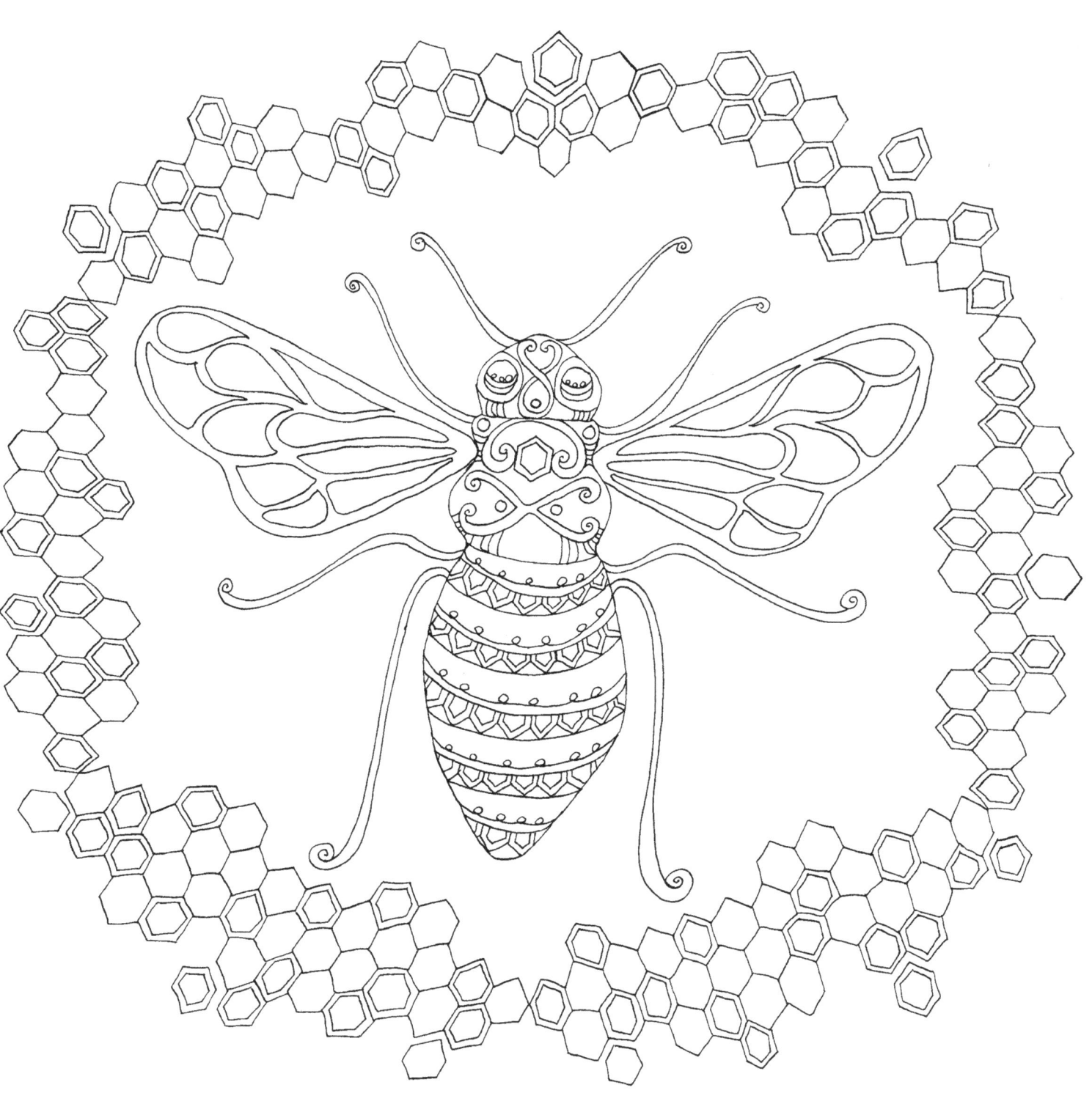

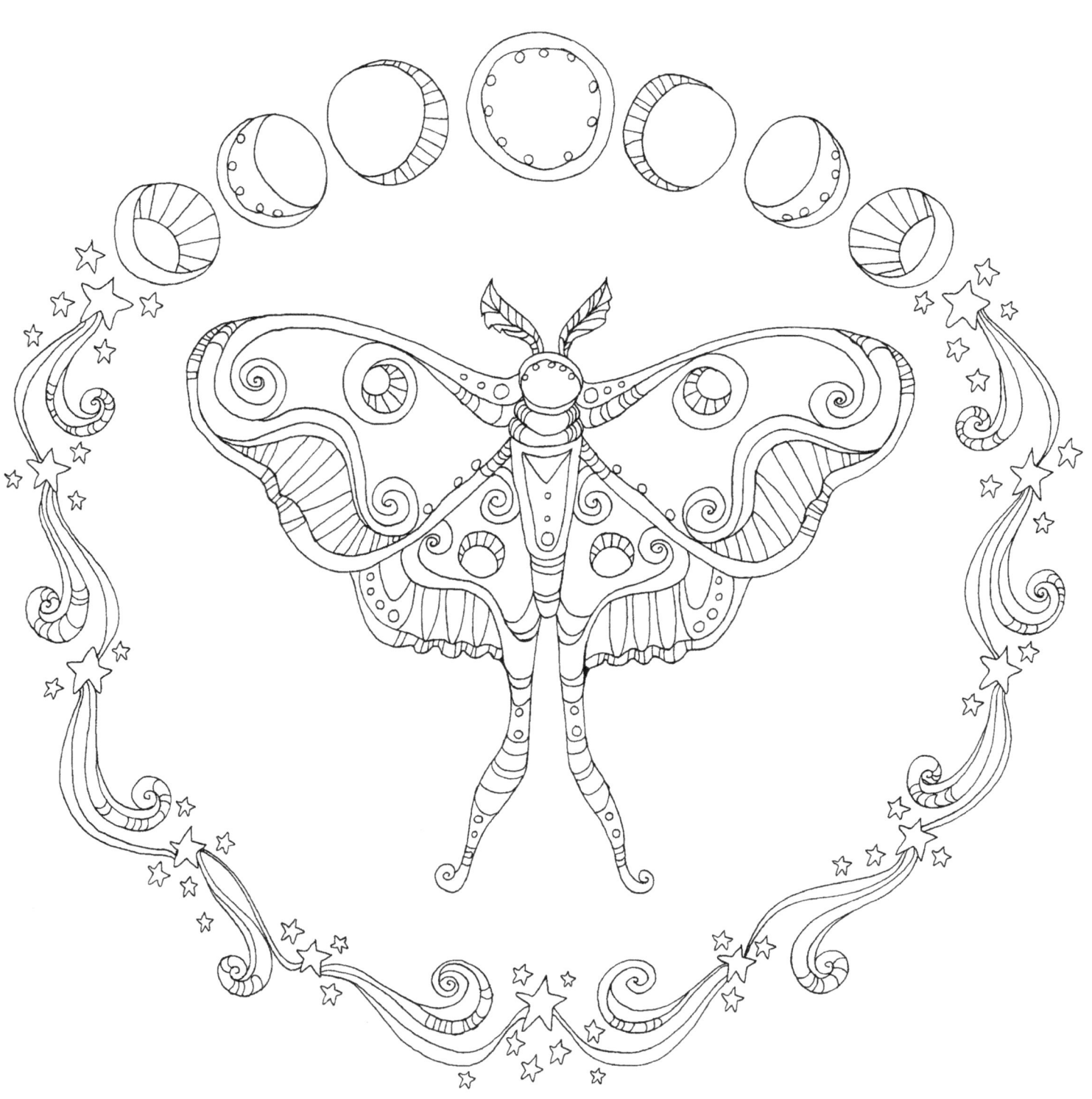

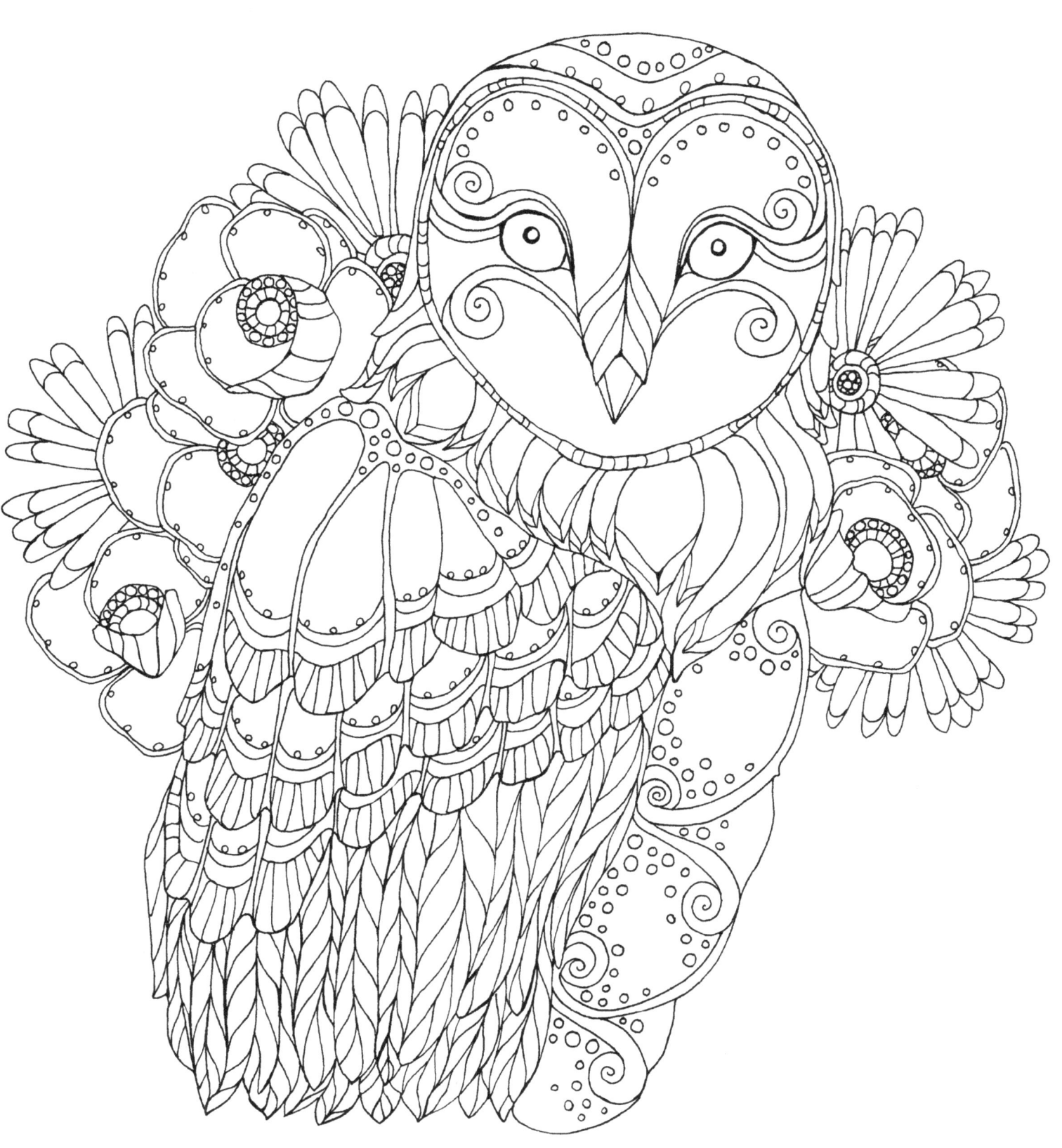

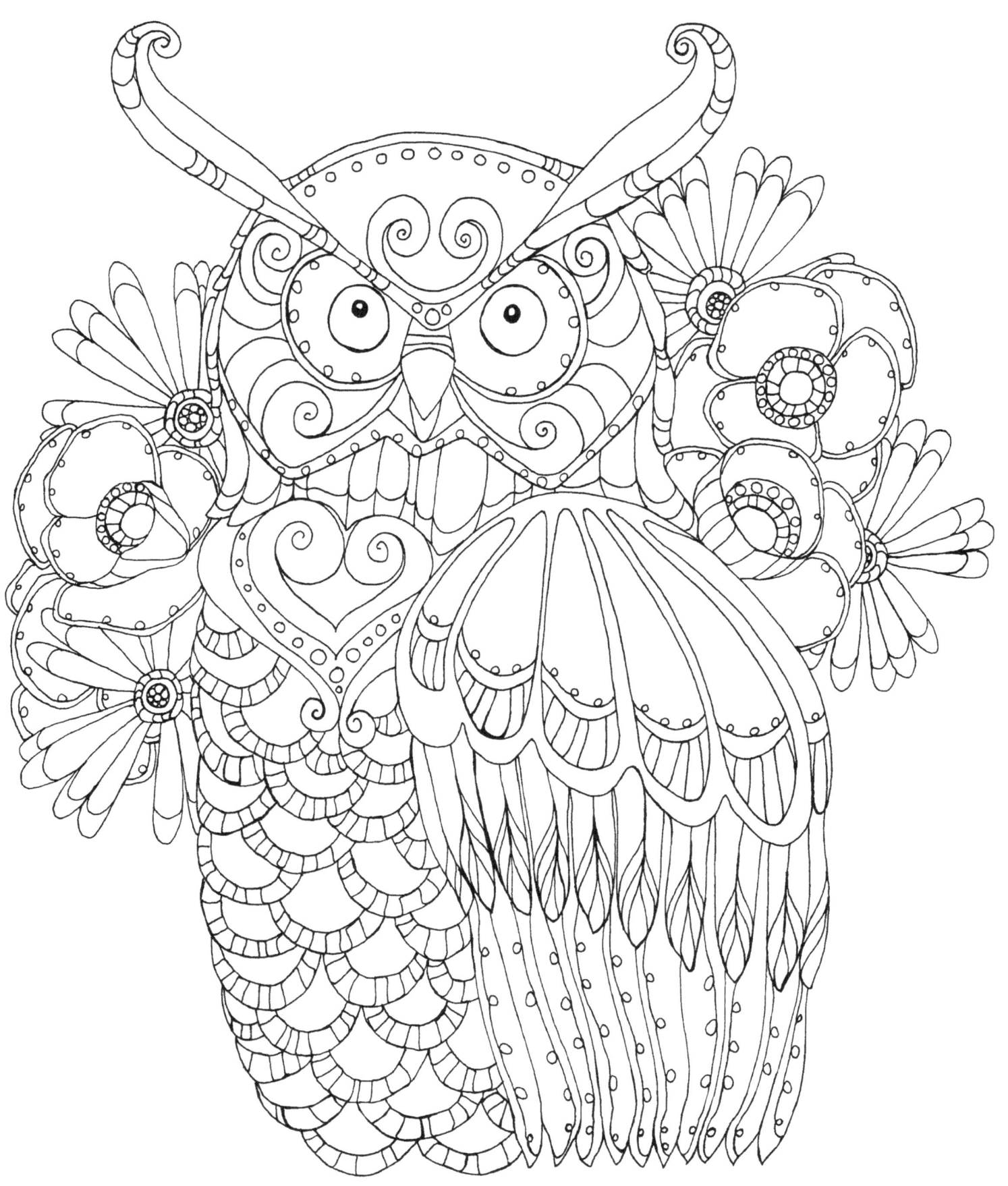

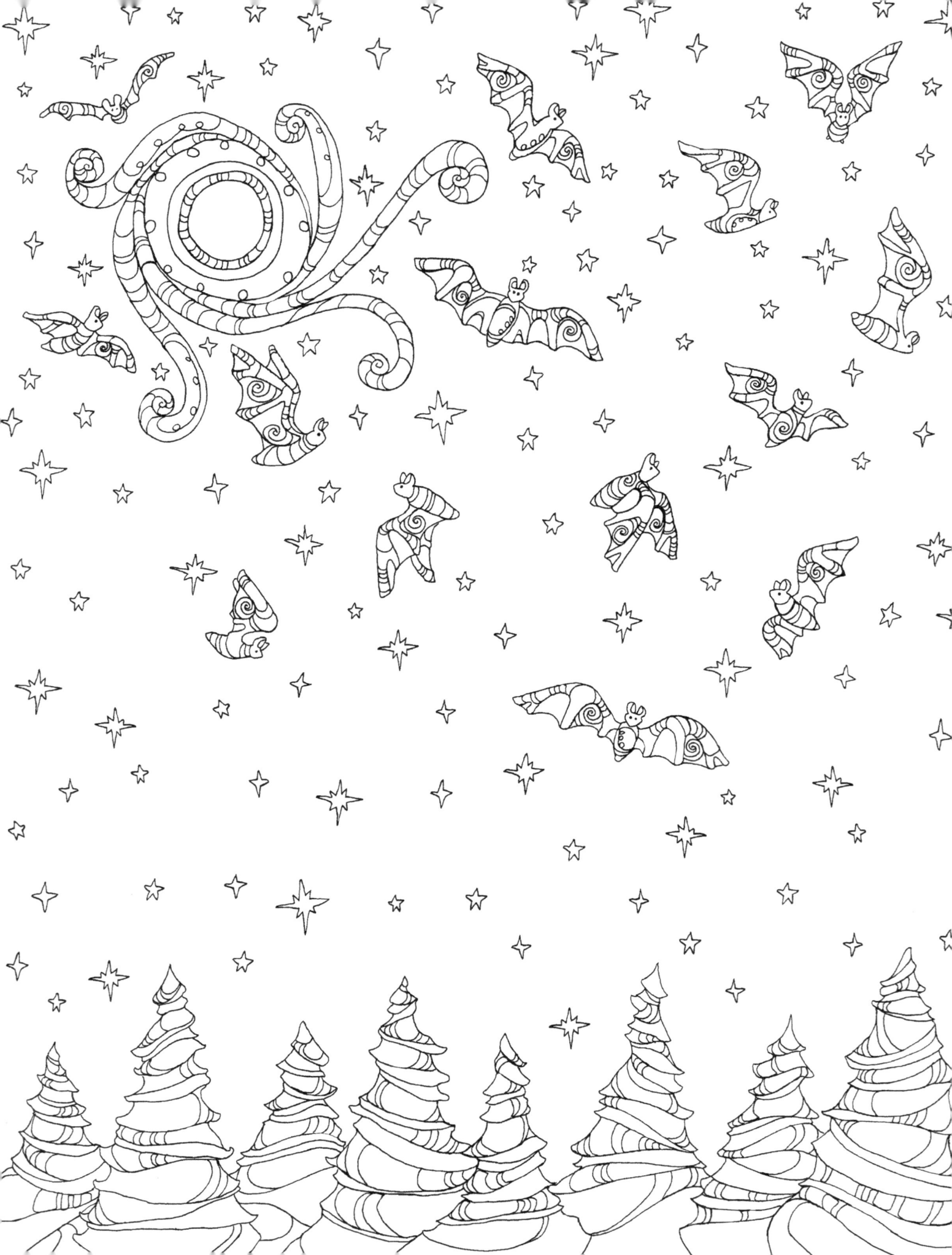

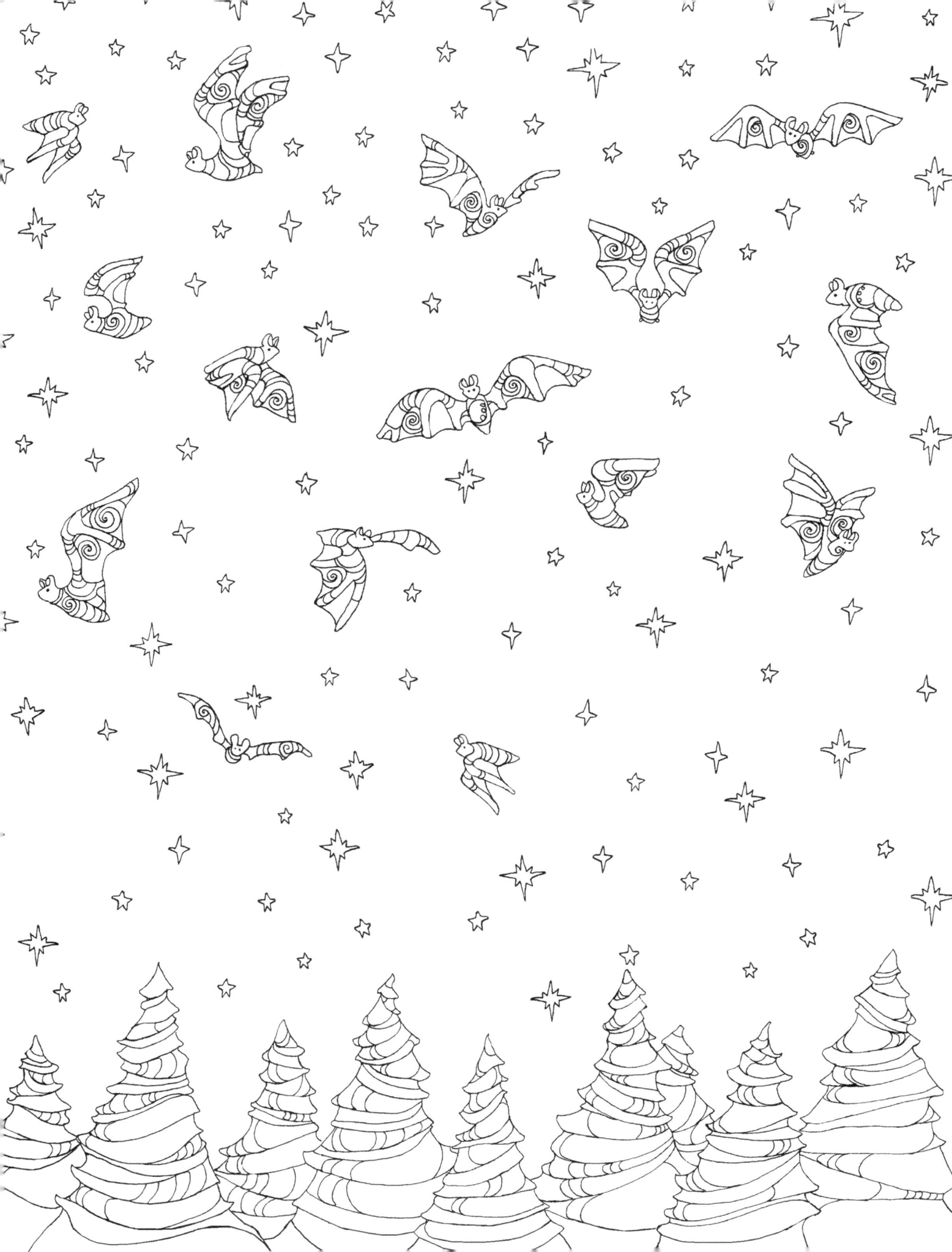

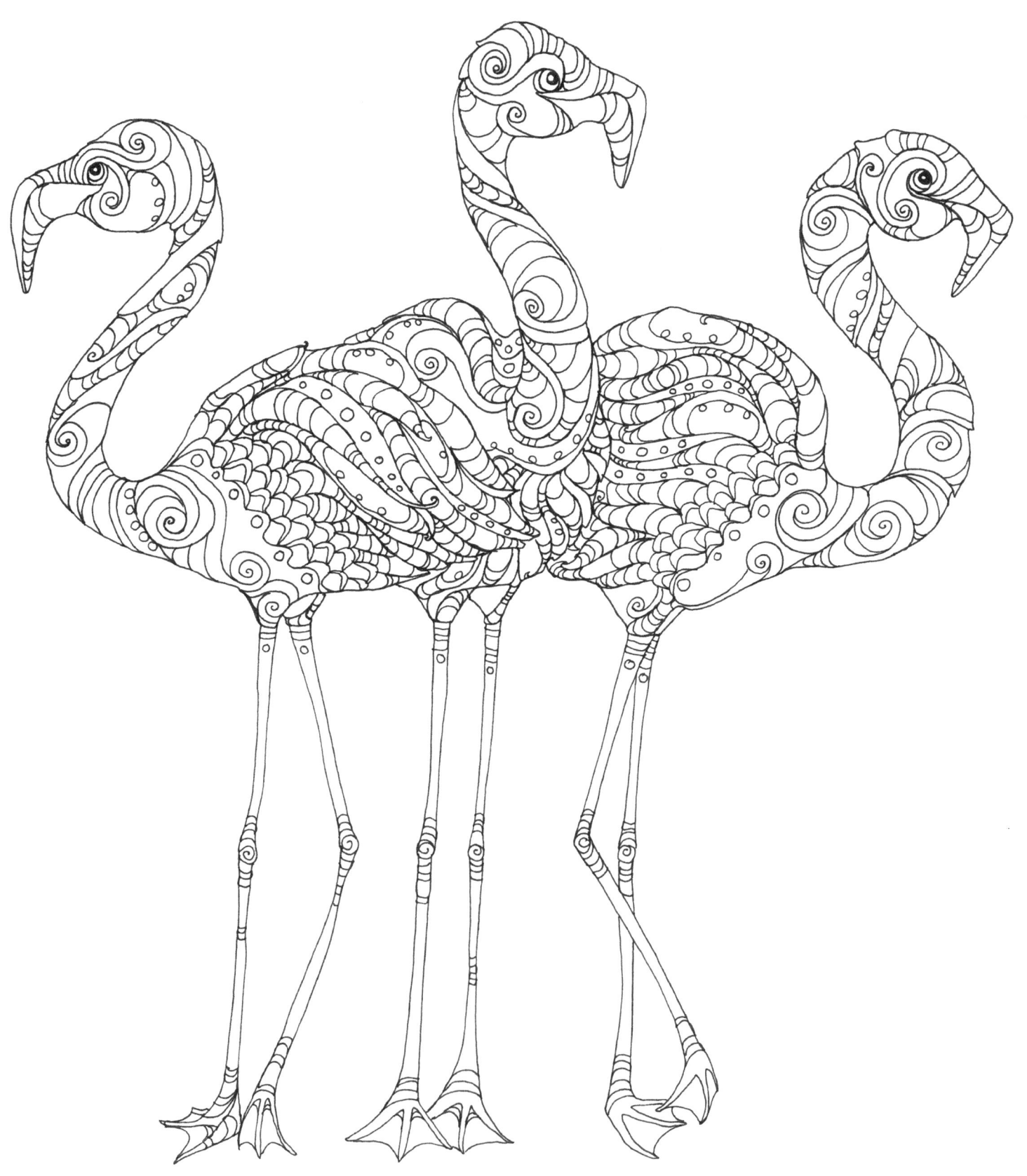

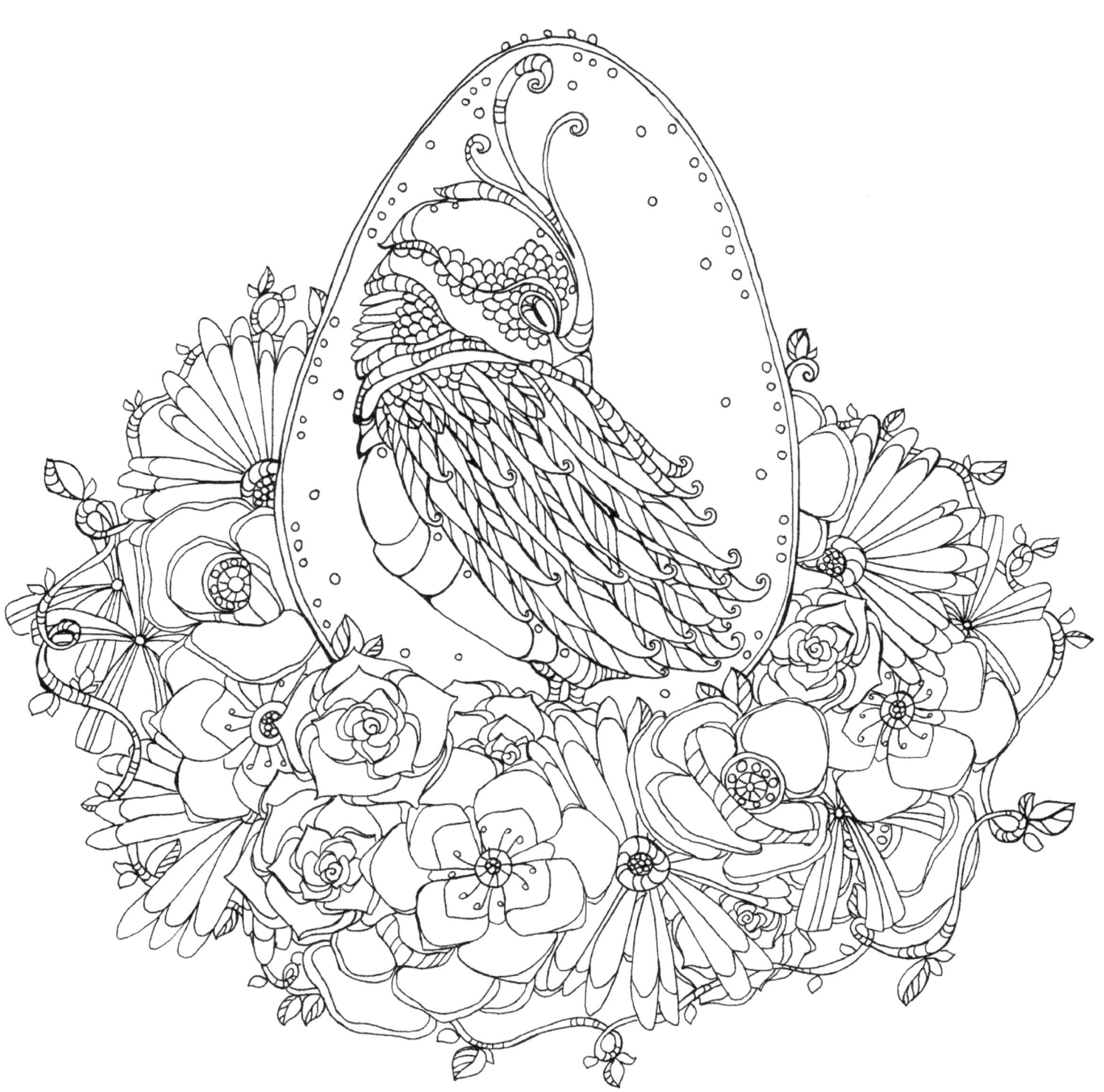

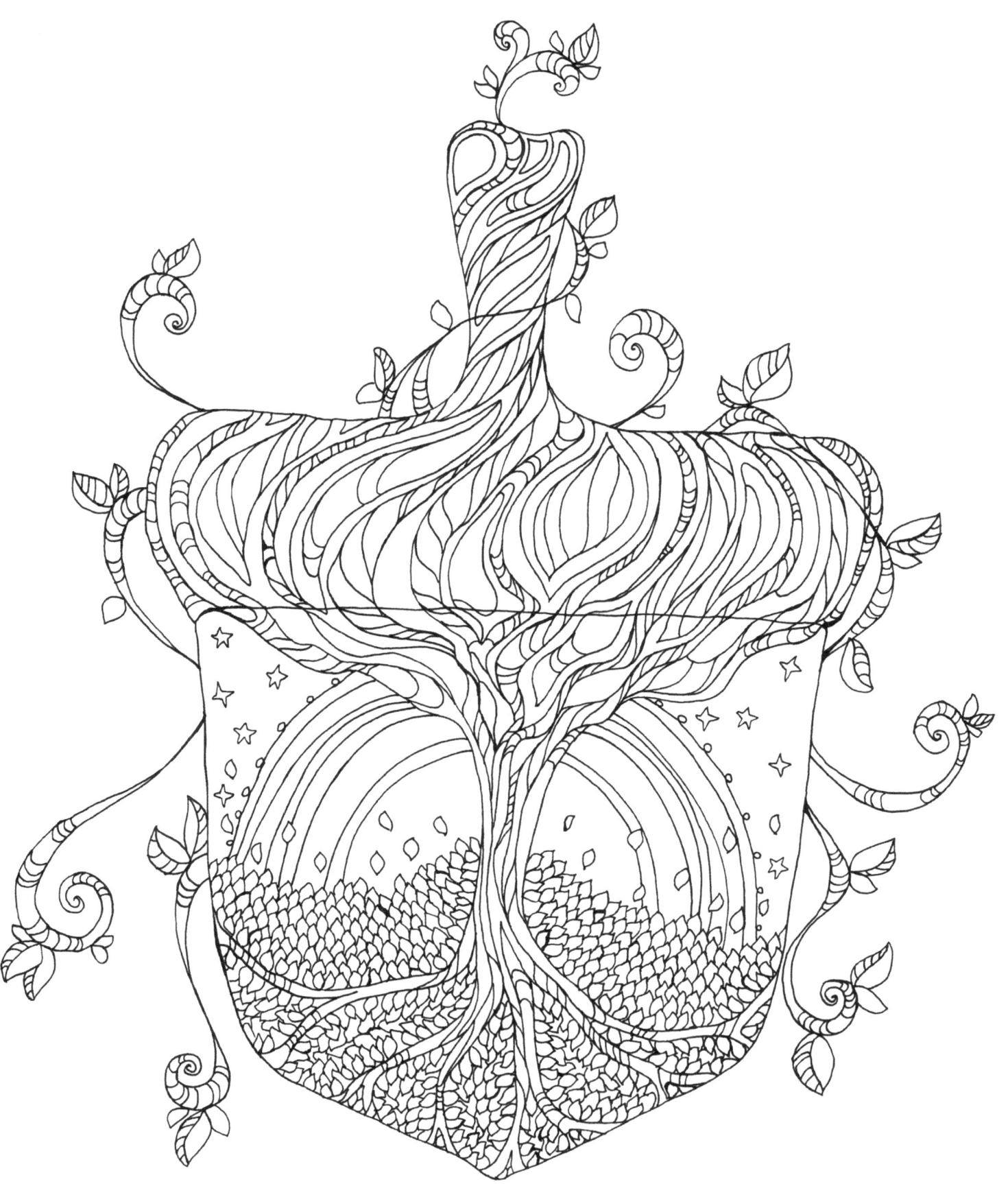

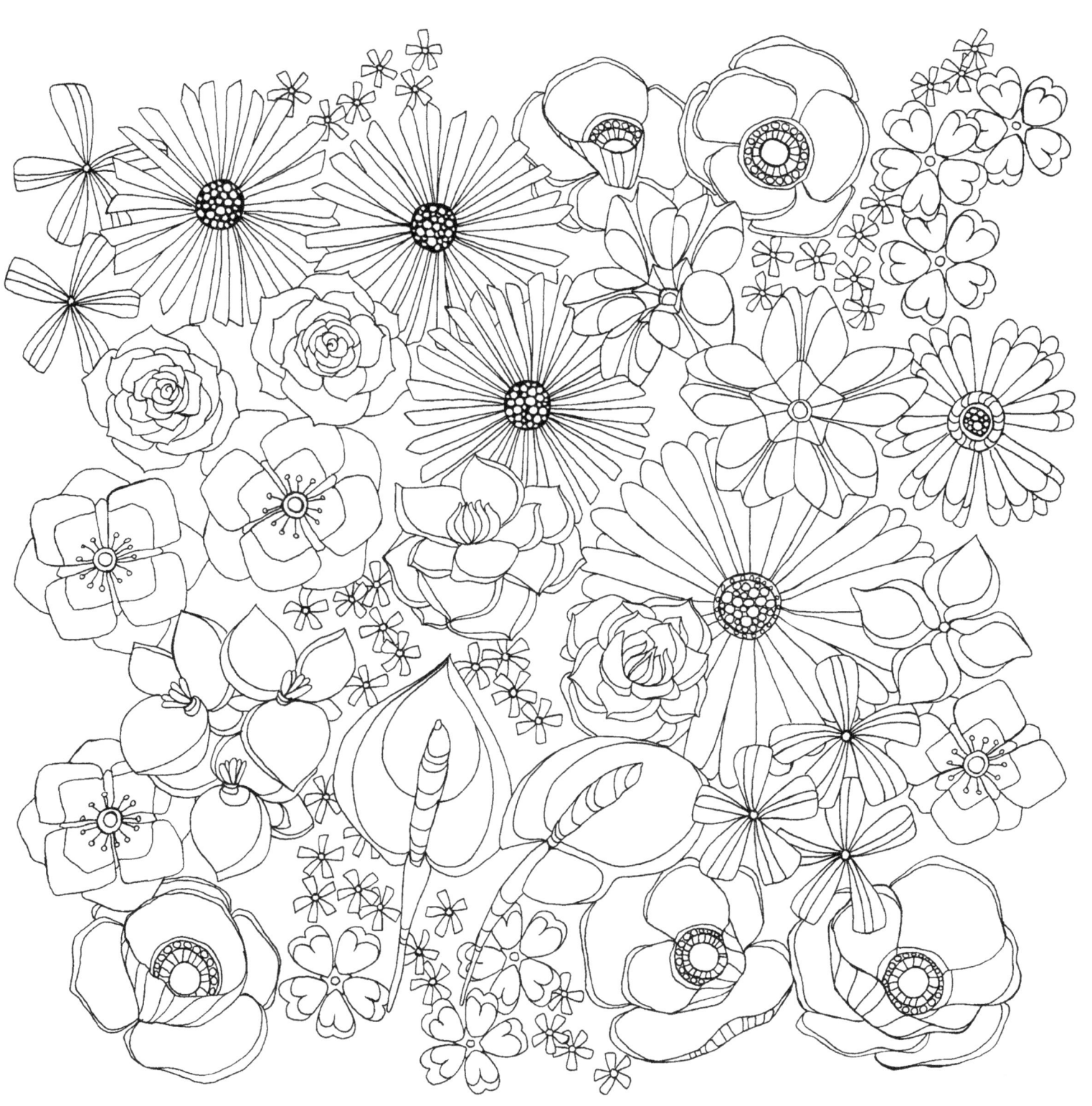

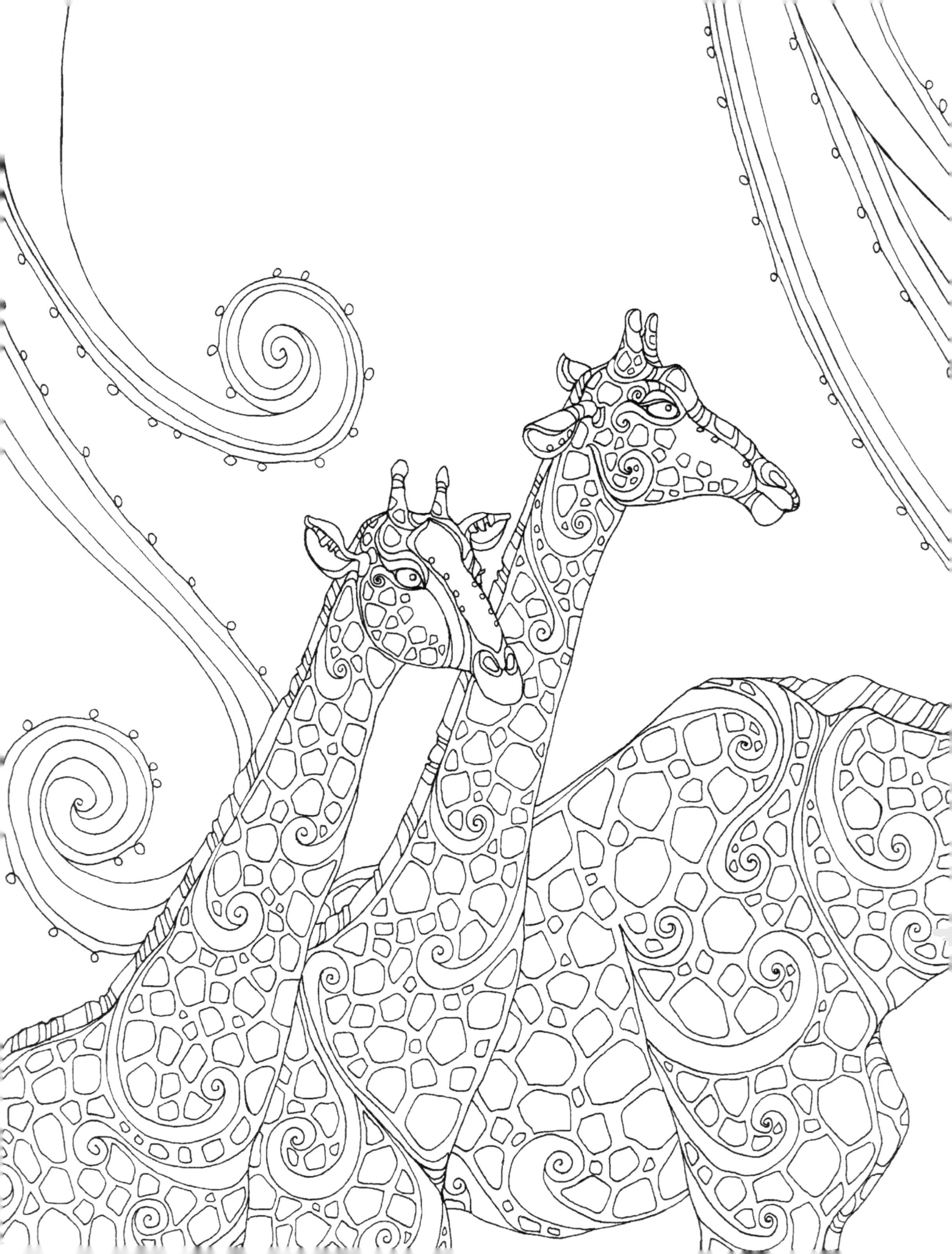

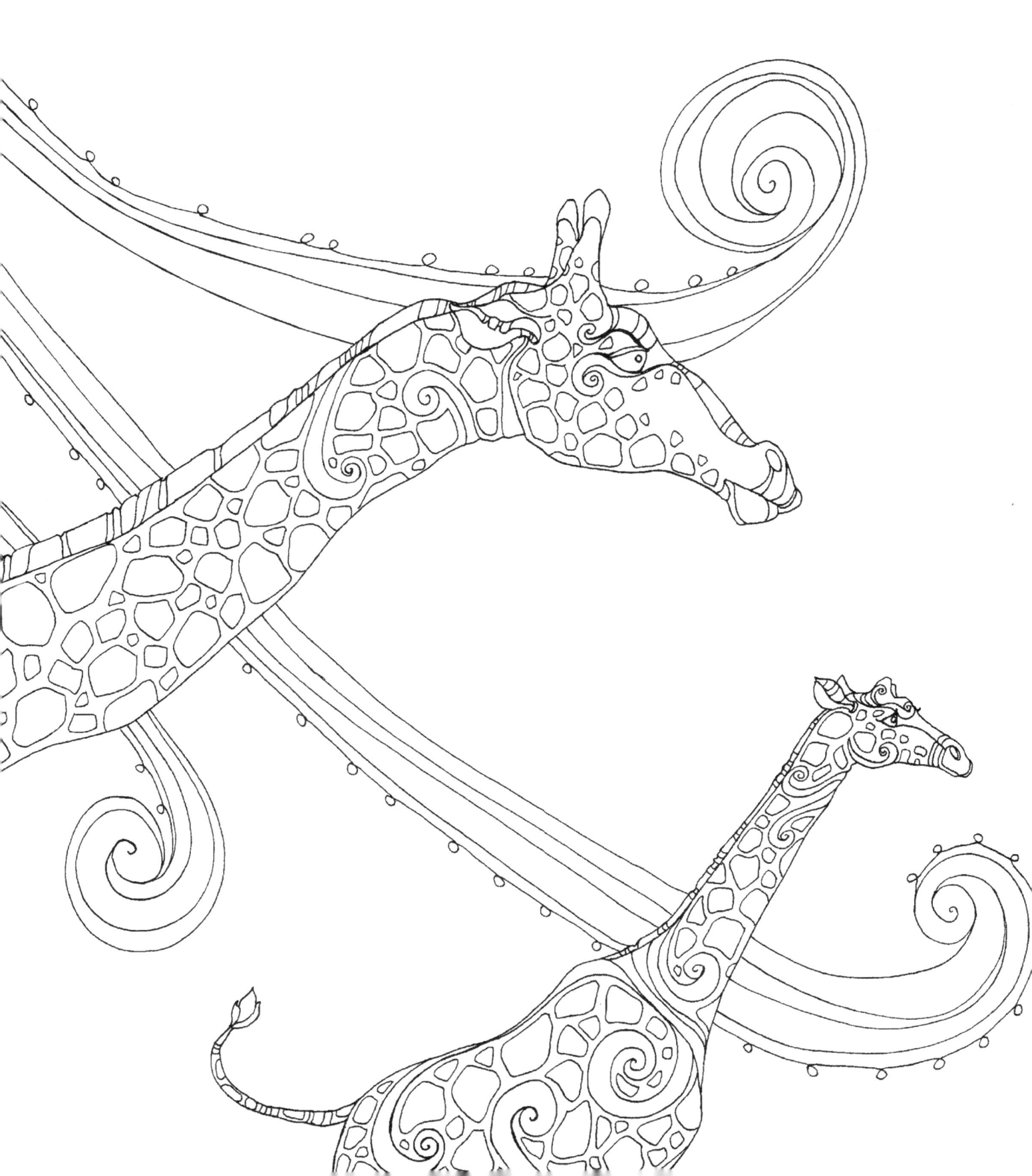

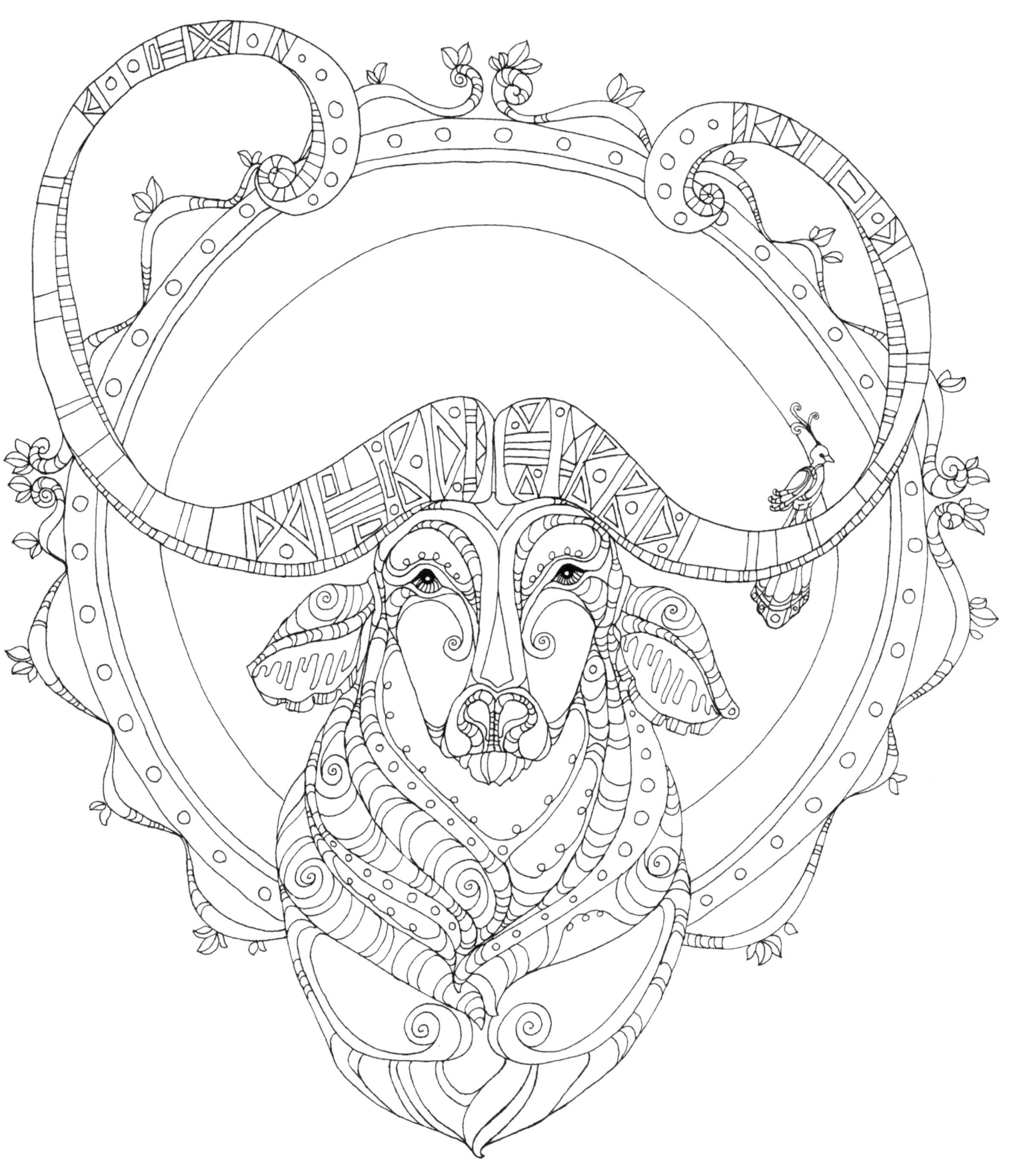

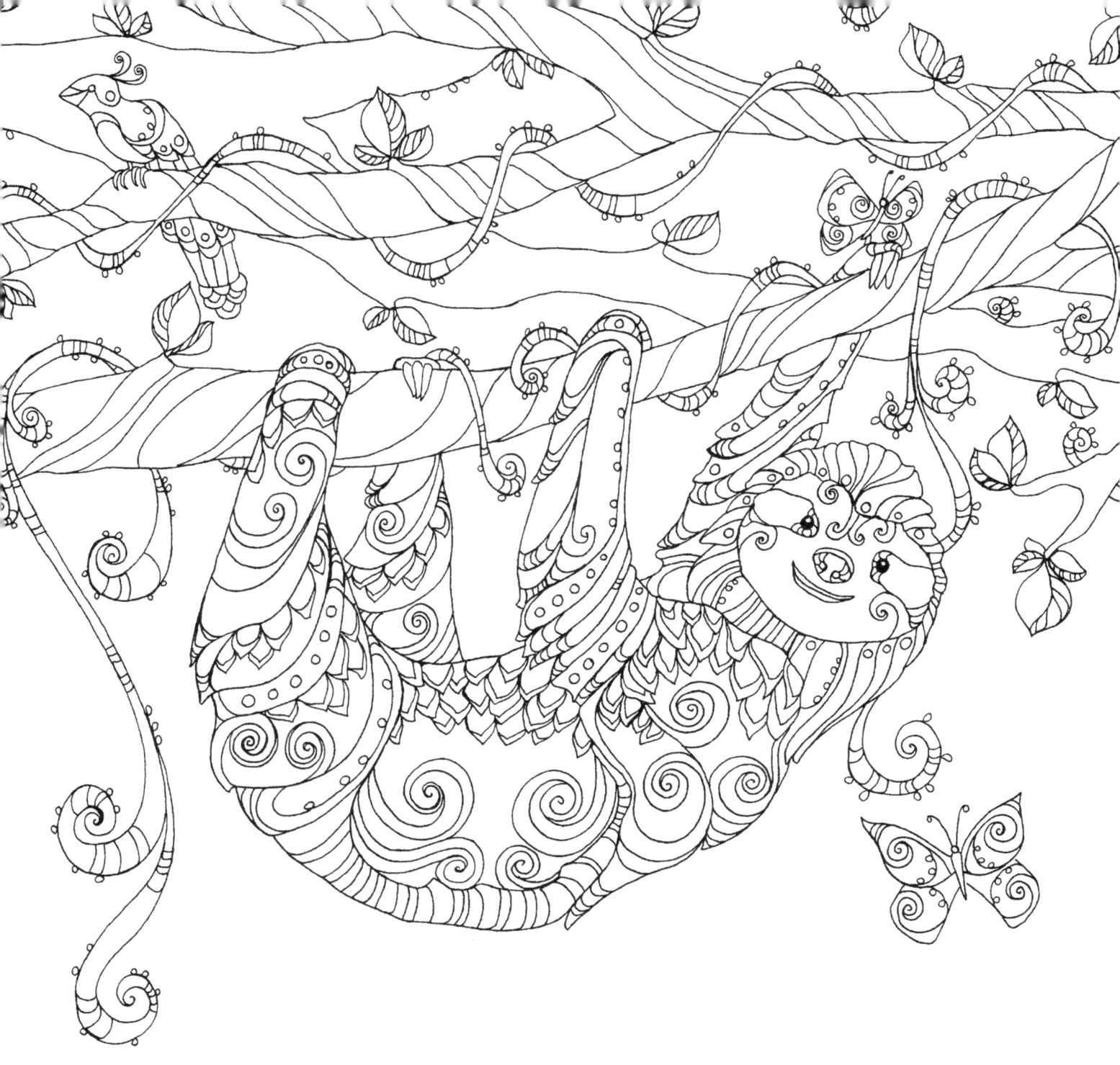

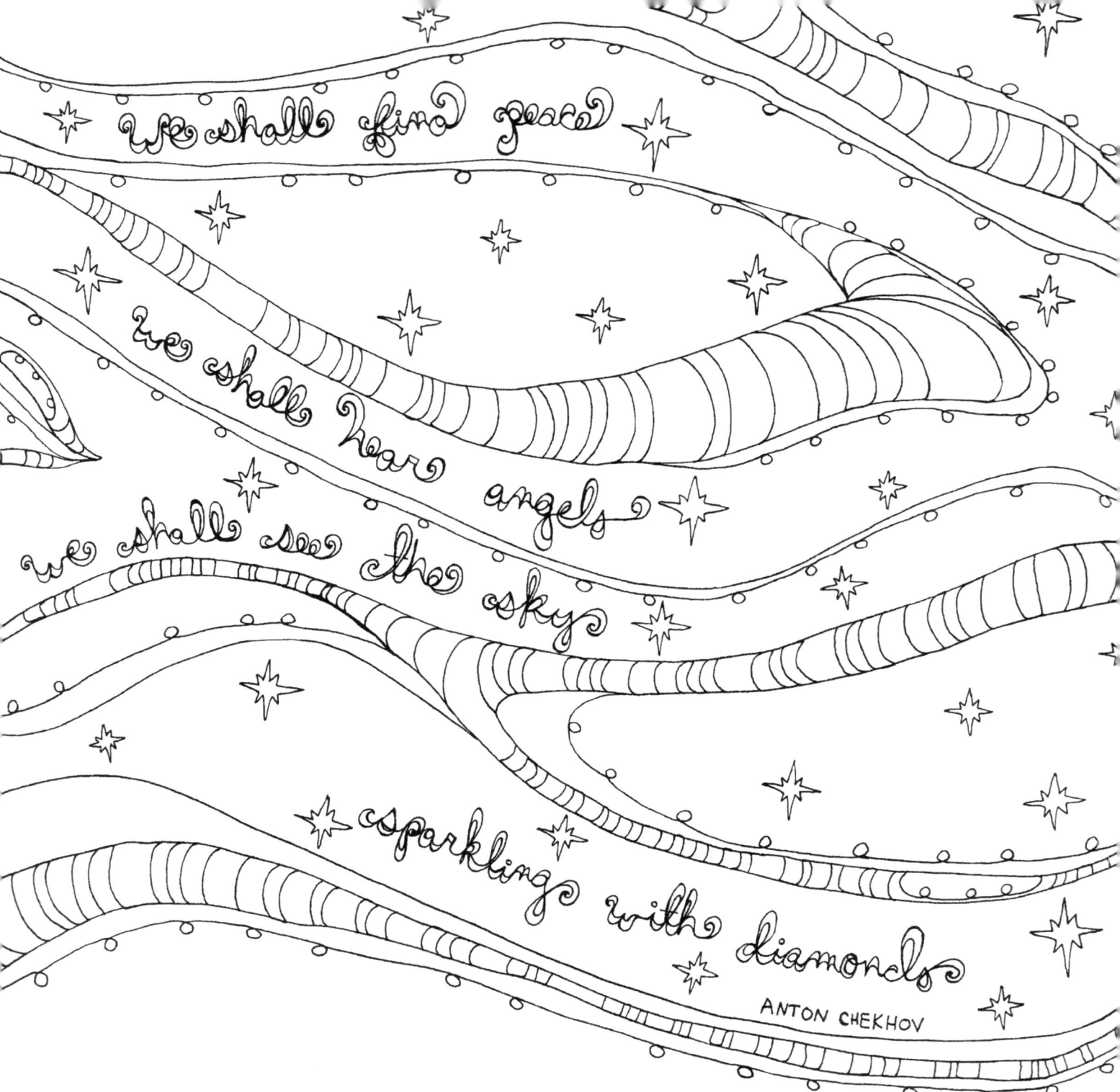

we shall find peace

we shall hear angels

we shall see the sky sparkling with diamonds

ANTON CHEKHOV

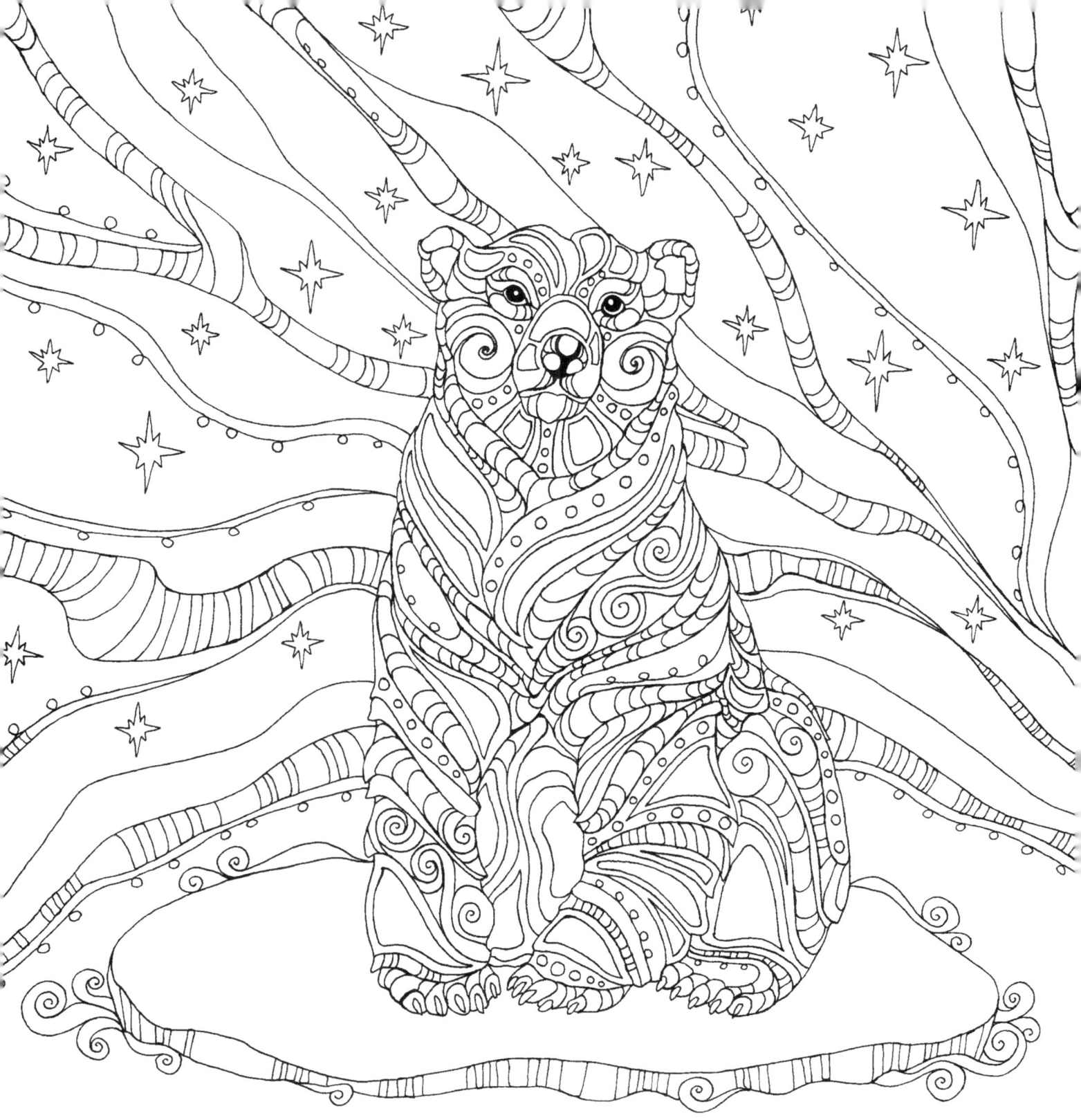

I'd love to see your work!
You can tag me on Instagram:
@peacelovemanatee

www.ingramcontent.com/pod-product-compliance
Lightning Source LLC
Chambersburg PA
CBHW050817180526
45159CB00004B/1701